Welcome

Welcome

Morris Greidanus
Arda Rooks
George Vander Velde

Bible Way
Grand Rapids, Michigan

Acknowledgments

This textbook—and the course by the same name—is the joint product of Morris Greidanus, pastor of First Christian Reformed Church, Grand Rapids, Michigan; Arda Rooks, English teacher at Toronto District Christian High; and George Vander Velde, professor of religion and theology at the Toronto Institute for Christian Studies. Lillian Grissen and the Education Department served as editors.

Library of Congress Cataloging in Publication Data
Greidanus, Morris.
   Welcome.

   1. Confirmation—Christian Reformed Church. 2. Christian Reformed Church—Doctrinal and controversial works. I. Rooks, Arnalda. II. Vander Velde, George. III. Title.
BX6826.G73   1982   234'.162   82-12907
ISBN 0-933140-48-7

5 4 3 2

Table of Contents

In the name of our Lord Jesus Christ, I now welcome you to all the privileges of full communion. I welcome you to full participation in the life of the church. I welcome you to its responsibilities, its joys, and its sufferings.

Form for Public Profession of Faith
Psalter Hymnal

Preface

You may be wondering about the title of this book. What exactly does *Welcome* mean? Does the church officially welcome people only after they have publicly professed their faith? The seven chapters of *Welcome* and the seven sessions of the *Welcome* course answer these questions and many more. *Welcome* aims to deepen your understanding of the act of confessing your faith in Jesus. It seeks to encourage the growth of both an intellectual understanding of the faith and commitment of heart and life to Jesus.

We ask that you read each chapter of *Welcome* at home before the class session. You'll notice that the study guide which concludes each chapter is divided into two sections, one to be completed At Home and the other In Class.

Please look for a moment at the study guide which follows chapter 1 (other chapters have similar study guides). The At Home section is usually divided into four parts: personal questions and comments, written assignment, additional reading, and Scripture reading. The In Class section contains provocative discussion questions, designed to clarify your ideas about profession of faith. Your instructor may choose to use some or all of these questions to guide your time together. However, your own questions are most important and should take precedence over any we've included in the study guide.

Before you begin reading *Welcome*, study the goals below and decide which of them seems most important to you.

1. To prepare you to make a meaningful profession of faith in Jesus Christ.
2. To help deepen your commitment so that you can make a more meaningful confession.

3. To help you understand the significance and the implications of your confession as a lifelong act of obedience.
4. To help you understand the privileges and responsibilities of confession.
5. To summarize for you the history, function, and purpose of profession of faith, and to explain its relationship to baptism and the Lord's Supper.
6. To equip you to make a statement of your faith before the consistory and/or congregation.

Take a few minutes now to reflect on your reasons for taking this course. We pray that the material presented here will help you as you contemplate this most important decision of your life.

Morris Greidanus
Arda Rooks
George Vander Velde

ONE

THE
CEREMONY

"Say, have you thought about making profession of faith* this year?" If you grew up in a churchgoing family, you've heard this question before. In fact you've probably heard it many times—from parents, from elders, from ministers, and from teachers. And you know how happy Mom and Dad will be when you tell them you've decided to confess your faith. They'll blink away a tear, quickly call Grandma and Grandpa, and say a prayer of thanksgiving. On the day you profess your faith before the congregation, people will smile at you and crush your hand warmly, and your family will act like it's your birthday.

That's the way it might be if you're part of a Christian family. But what if you're not? If you became a Christian recently, the suggestion "You should publicly profess your faith" may have puzzled you. Hm-m, *public* profession? What's that? You've already said clearly and shown in various ways that you believe in Christ. Why this ceremony?

That's an appropriate question. The church is convinced that it's important for you to profess your faith publicly. Members of the church expect it; parents hope for it; elders and ministers ask about it; there's even a special form for it in the back of the *Psalter Hymnal*, the church hymnbook.

What is this act, this public profession?

Maybe you think everybody, at least all church members, understands the ceremony of public profession of faith. Not so. Many believe one or more myths about profession of faith.

*Some folks call it *profession* of faith. Others call it *confession* of faith. *Profession* or *confession*, it refers to the same action.

10

Before you make public profession, you should not only look at some of these myths but also explore the meaning and implications of public profession. Perhaps a good way to begin is to consider what public profession is *not*.

What Profession of Faith Is Not

It's not graduation. At times young people look at profession of faith as a graduation ceremony, a way of wrapping up those long years of catechism. When the last catechism book is finished, they reason, it's time to graduate.

Actually, the Christian never graduates. The Bible pictures the Christian life as continuous growth in the knowledge of the Lord. That means adults have just as much responsibility to continue studying and learning as young people do.

So if you're planning to publicly profess your faith because "everybody's doing it" or because you're tired of studying, think it over. You need a much better reason.

It's not just one more hurdle. Sometimes baptized members want to profess their faith so they may be married in church, have the baby baptized, or take part in the Lord's Supper. The relationship of profession of faith to these ceremonies and sacraments is complicated, but you need to see that profession of faith is much more than just a hurdle you must clear to reach the Lord's table. Profession is a joyful, meaningful sign that faith is real. *When* you have that faith, profess it—publicly—in front of fellow believers.

It's not only for the perfect. You already know you aren't perfect. You also know you don't *have* to be morally perfect before you profess your faith. What you might not know is that publicly professing your faith won't make it easier to live the Christian life. In fact, you might have to struggle against sin even more than you did before.

In confessing your faith, you're not claiming to be close to perfection. You're admitting—publicly—that you are a sinner who needs God's grace. You're telling the Christian community that you know Jesus Christ is the only one who can help you break with sin and renew your life. And you're dedicating your whole life to Jesus.

It's not the third sacrament. Even though you'll find a form for it in the back of the *Psalter Hymnal*, profession of faith is not a sacrament. All churches do not agree on the number of sacraments: for example, the Roman Catholic Church has seven. But the Christian Reformed Church believes that only two sacraments are clearly commanded in the Bible: the Lord's

Supper and baptism. The sacrament of infant baptism, accepted for you by your parents, makes you a baptized member of the church. If you were not baptized as a baby, then baptism and public profession together become one beautiful ceremony.

What Profession of Faith Is

Public profession of faith is the mature answer to God's grace, God's amazing magnetic power to draw people (who don't deserve God's goodness at all) to the point you are now considering—professing your belief in Jesus Christ.

When you profess your faith, you say for all to hear, "God's love is present in my life." You are telling the congregation, "I want to join you in responding to his love with my life."

It isn't hard to see why this ceremony means so much to Christian parents, is it? It shows that you are responding to their upbringing. You know your own heart; you know your personal relationship to God. You are ready to stand on your own feet—with God's help. And you want to be a partner in the church's work of proclaiming God's grace. Fellow Christians now see you as a mature, responsible church member. In a sense, profession of faith marks a person's passage from childhood into adulthood.

Almost all cultures mark the passage from childhood into adulthood with some sort of ritual or rite. Some, like the American Indian, expected boys to pass certain tests of bravery and endurance before they were considered men. Others, like our own society, use age as the marker: when young people reach a certain age, they may drink, vote, or run for office— they're adults. Acts like getting a driver's license become rituals.

But most religions are reluctant to measure a person's maturity by age alone: knowledge of faith and commitment to its ways are equally important. So religious rites-of-passage rituals usually involve a display of adult knowledge and religious maturity. On the Sabbath nearest his thirteenth birthday, at a ceremony known as bar mitzvah, a Jewish boy celebrates arriving at the age of religious responsibility. He is expected to recite the Ten Commandments, to proclaim the blessing before and after the reading of the Law, and to read and translate a section of the Hebrew Law.

Although the New Testament doesn't mention an identical ceremony, Jesus, when he was only twelve years old, did meet with the teachers of the Law in that amazing session that resembled bar mitzvah. And Timothy, we're told, made the "good confession in the presence of many witnesses" (1 Tim. 6:12, NIV).

History of Profession of Faith

Early in the Christian era the Roman Catholic Church considered confirmation a sacrament. At the age of seven—after being instructed in the faith—children were confirmed, or admitted, to full membership in the church. These confirmed children, said the church, were equipped with the Holy Spirit to battle sin.

The Reformers, however, rejected the sacrament of confirmation. They believed that infants received the Holy Spirit when they were baptized, not seven years later at a confirmation ceremony. They insisted that confirmation should be replaced with catechism instruction.

Why this change? John Calvin believed young members should know the Apostles' Creed, the Law, the Lord's Prayer, and the part of the catechism dealing with the Lord's Supper before they could meaningfully take part in the sacrament. Just as law students are admitted to the bar only after they have passed their examinations, so ten-year-olds in Calvin's time were admitted to the Lord's Supper after passing a test.

It seems strange to us that ten-year-olds of Calvin's day had already acquired enough learning about creeds and catechism to satisfy Calvin's emphasis on knowledge. What has happened since Calvin's day that should make the Christian Reformed Church so cautious about early profession of faith? Don't today's ten-year-olds know as much about creeds and catechism as the ten-year-olds of Calvin's day?

Probably. But although, like Calvin, we believe knowledge is important, we also stress commitment. The two are closely tied. *Knowledge* is that intellectual understanding of the belief or faith being confessed. *Commitment* is the heart-and-life response of that faith.

It's because of this double emphasis that most ten-year-olds in our church do not make public profession. Although they might have the knowledge, they are seldom mature enough to make the full commitment and as a result are not mature enough to partake of the Lord's Supper.

The Christian Reformed Church Order (1916–1965), Article 61, stated it this way:

> None shall be admitted to the Lord's Supper except those who according to the usage of the church with which they unite themselves have made a confession of the Reformed religion, besides being reputed to

be of a godly walk, without which those who come from other Churches shall not be admitted.

The formulary used for profession of faith in the Christian Reformed Church since 1972 (Appendix II) also stresses the importance of both knowledge and commitment. It explicitly asks for agreement with the teachings and government of the church, commitment to work with the church, and a personal statement of faith.

And What About You?

In the next few weeks we will struggle together to discover the meaning of profession of faith. We are not asking you to make a decision now—only to commit yourself to working through this course. When, or perhaps even before, you have finished studying this book, you should be better equipped to decide whether you are ready to publicly profess your faith in Jesus Christ.

STUDY
GUIDE

At Home

1. My comments/questions on chapter one

2. Think about (and jot down in the margins) some prevalent attitudes and practices surrounding the ceremony of profession of faith in your congregation. Some of the following questions may be helpful:

   a. What's the average age of persons making profession of faith in your congregation?

   b. What seems to motivate people, especially young people, to profess their faith?

    c. Are persons over twenty who haven't made profession of faith stigmatized in any way?

    d. How would the consistory of your church react if a twelve-year-old wanted to make profession of faith? How would the congregation react? How would you react?

3. John Calvin wrote some interesting and insightful things about profession of faith. If you'd like to read what he has to say, see Appendix III, Section A.

4. For your Scripture reading this week see Colossians 1:3–14 (especially verses 9 and 10) and 2:1–6 (especially verses 6 and 7). Paul compares our growth in Christ to a plant's roots growing firmly in the soil. As a plant depends on the soil, so we depend on Christ to grow. Profession of faith reflects this growth in Christ—it is neither the beginning nor the end of Christian living.

In Class

1. May the profession of faith ceremony be compared to a rite of passage from childhood to adulthood? If so, should a twelve-year-old be permitted to make profession of faith? Why or why not?

2. Why is profession of faith not considered a sacrament in the Christian Reformed Church? Should it be?

3. In your congregation do the practices surrounding profession of faith reflect a healthy balance of head knowledge and heart commitment? If possible, explain your answer with examples.

TWO

THE MEANING
OF CONFESSION

Do you *confess* your faith or do you *profess* it? Which is the right word?

The church's forms for public profession of faith use both words. The 1972 form prevents a giggle by saying, "The questions may be changed into statements and said by the *confessors.*" We reserve the noun *professor* for the academic world.

If you'll look at the verbs *confess* and *profess* in your dictionary, you'll find similar definitions. Both verbs mean "to declare, to make known." It's useful to have both terms because each emphasizes a different aspect of this declaration. To *confess* has a suggestion of "to say *with*"; you don't say your confession alone but *with* the church and *with* Jesus. To *profess* has the element of "to say *before*"; the statement you make is a public act.

The New Testament Greek word *homologein*, "to say the same thing," is translated variously in the Bible: "to confess," "to profess," "to acknowledge," "to witness." It has a legal tone, the flavor of official testimony given in a court of law. As such, it stands in contrast to denying something (cf. John 1:20).

But the essential meaning of the word is religious, related to declaring our faith in Jesus Christ as Savior and Lord. Paul clearly uses *homologein* in that sense when he tells us, ". . . if you confess with your lips that Jesus is Lord and believe in your heart that God raised him from the dead, you will be saved" (Rom. 10:9). The early church shortened that into the simple confession, "Jesus is Lord!"

So whether we use the term *public profession* or *confession of faith*, we mean the act of stating what we believe, who our

Savior is, and whom we promise to serve loyally as our Lord.

A Public Faith

The link Paul makes between confession and salvation shows how important it is to come out in the open with your beliefs. In fact, there is no salvation without confession. If that sounds too heavy, think of it this way: to be saved you must believe, and no one will ever know what you believe if you don't say it.

You might argue that even when you hide your faith from your friends, or when it doesn't show in your whole life, God sees it because he sees in secret. But there is no such thing as a secret faith. God wants others to see your faith. Jesus says:

> . . .every one who acknowledges [confesses] me
> before men, I also will acknowledge before my Father
> who is in heaven; but whoever denies me before men,
> I also will deny before my Father who is in heaven.
>
> (Matt. 10:32, 33)

When you openly tell others that Jesus is your Lord, Jesus openly tells God that you belong to him. But, the opposite is also true. If you can't be bothered with Jesus in public, if you deny him in the way you talk and act, then he doesn't know you either:

> For whoever is ashamed of me and of my words in
> this adulterous and sinful generation, of him will the
> Son of man also be ashamed, when he comes in the
> glory of his Father with the holy angels.
>
> (Mark 8:38)

The key to what *denial* means is the phrase "ashamed of me and my words." When we deny Jesus, we keep him in the background of our lives and don't permit his words to guide what we do. When we *confess* Jesus, on the other hand, we say that he is Lord and we live by his words.

Confession is far easier for twentieth-century Christians than it was for New Testament Christians. When we confess our faith publicly, our relatives usually approve, the church receives us warmly, and the church community stands with us in living the obedient, confessing life. For us, confession brings security, approval, and warmth. For New Testament Christians, confession frequently brought fear, disapproval, and even death. These Christians faced the disapproval of Jewish relatives and the hostility of a Roman society that confessed Caesar as Lord. Confessing their faith could cost them their necks. Many paid that price; they were martyred for their faith. In fact, the Greek word translated as "witness" is *marturein*, which means, "to be a martyr, to witness."

17

Because of these dangers, some of those early believers decided confession was simply too risky and kept their faith hidden. They saw his signs, they heard his words, they believed he was right. But they tried the impossible: to combine faith in Jesus and a good rating with Jesus' despisers. John concludes sadly: "... they loved the praise of men more than the praise of God" (John 12:43).

A Living Faith

If you are beginning to think that there is more to confessing your faith than merely standing a single time in front of the congregation to say you believe in Jesus Christ, you're catching on. Of course, *confession of faith* does mean knowing what you believe and saying the right words before God and his people. But it means so much more; it means living by those words, putting your deeds where your mouth is. For Christians who "profess to know God, but ... deny him by their deeds ... are detestable, disobedient, unfit for any good deed" (Titus 1:16).

If you confess Christ as your Lord, your life will reflect your confession; your deeds will match your words. You will try to be meek in a world that prizes aggressiveness. You will vote for certain social policies because Jesus commands you to love your neighbor. You will hang on to the Lord by faith even though your sickness or suffering (or that of a person dear to you) at times makes you doubt his promises. You will hang in there by faith no matter what.

No one can predict what denials Christians may face or in which situations they may have to shout: "Wait a minute! My Lord says...." No one can foresee how hard it may become to develop Christian alternatives on the big social and public issues, nor how repressive government policies might become, even in democratic societies. But the Lord says about those who hang in there by faith no matter what:

> He who conquers shall be clad thus in white garments, and I will not blot his name out of the book of life; I will confess his name before my Father and before his angels.
>
> (Rev. 3:5)

It's an adventurous life, this life of confessing, of conquering, of spotting denials, of listening for Jesus' voice. That public act before the congregation is just a beginning. It's a step on the road that begins when you first acknowledge your faith in Jesus. You tell your friends and your parents. You confess before the consistory and the congregation that you know him. And after that the profession continues; you keep on confessing your Lord "before men" until he returns and every knee bows to him and everyone confesses him as Lord.

Fear of Commitment

Where do average persons get the nerve to pledge themselves to a life of faith and ongoing commitment?

Through the strength of Jesus Christ. The apostle Paul reminds us that Christ Jesus made the good confession before Pontius Pilate in the presence of many witnesses (John 18:37, 1 Tim. 6:13). That confession cost Jesus his life—and led to his victory.

Through the Holy Spirit, that strength to confess and conquer may be ours. The Holy Spirit helps us believe that Jesus is Lord. The Holy Spirit teaches us to pray to God as Father. The Holy Spirit helps us say (or profess) what needs to be said (Matt. 10:16–20; Gal. 4:6, 7; 1 John 5:1).

With that kind of help we needn't be afraid. We can confess Jesus as Lord and live each day as his disciples.

STUDY
GUIDE

At Home

1. My comments/questions on chapter two

2. To prepare for next week's class session, interview an elderly church member or a member who has just recently confessed his or her faith. Ask what the phrase "confessing is a lifelong task" means and in what ways the person experiences the struggles of living his or her profession.

   Be ready to summarize your interview for the class at its next session.

3. For additional reading this week, study the Form for Public Profession of Faith (Appendix II).

4. For your devotions this week, read Matthew 10:16–20 and John 14:25–27 to discover the comfort of Christ's promise that he will never leave you to live your confession alone.

In Class

1. What differences of meaning are suggested by *confess* and *profess*?

2. Compare the use of these terms in the 1959 Form for Public Profession of Faith (*Psalter Hymnal*) with the 1972 form (Appendix II). What conclusions can you draw about the words *profess* and *confess* from the way they are used in these forms?

3. What are the two basic meanings of "confessing our faith"? In other words, what two things does confession involve?

4. "Confession as a lifelong task" is a major theme of this chapter and of the Bible itself. Drawing on the interview you completed last week (see question 2 of At Home), discuss these questions:

   a. How does confessing Christ involve all areas of our lives?

   b. How does living a confession sometimes become a real struggle? Give some examples.

   c. Do you personally have doubts or concerns about the tremendous impact which the confession "Jesus is Lord" should have on your life?

5. After drifting through four years of doubt, apathy, cynicism, and even unbelief, Bert is quite sure that he loves and believes in the Lord. Yet he does not feel ready to make public profession of faith. He feels he needs more time to let his commitment grow and more time to find out what faith is all about.

   What advice would you give Bert? Should he, for example, be urged to profess his faith, lest he be denied by Christ for having only a secret faith (see Matt. 10:32–33)? Or should he be advised to wait until he feels ready?

THREE

THE FAITH CONFESSED

The church was quiet as the young man stood up. The people had heard hundreds of public professions over the years, but today's was special. Dan Adams had never attended catechism with others his age. Dan Adams seldom understood much of the preacher's sermon either. Dan Adams had mental impairments.

The minister left his podium and went to stand by Dan. He read no forms, quoted no Scripture. In his gentle voice, he asked simply, "Dan, do you love Jesus?" Dan smiled eagerly. He nodded. "Yes," he said, "yes!"

In that one word, "yes," Dan made the most important confession of his life. And for Dan that one word was enough. But how about the rest of us? How many words and sentences and paragraphs must we use to profess our faith?

The New Testament teaches us that statements of faith don't have to be long. In fact, the Bible records many short statements of faith: God is light; God is love; Jesus is the Christ; Jesus Christ has come in the flesh; Jesus is the Son of God; Jesus is Lord. Apparently, the important thing is that we confess our faith, not that we use a lot of words to do it.

Of course, even a few brief words can have tremendous implications. The phrase "Jesus is Lord" was, at one time, radical and dangerous. That simple, short statement of loyalty to Jesus contradicted the Roman faith that Caesar was Lord—and the empire could and would strike back.

But, in spite of that danger, the early church expected all believers to make such a statement. The apostle Peter had provided a model. When Jesus asked him, "Who do you think I am?" Peter didn't hesitate. He confessed, "You are the Christ, the Son of the living God" (Matt. 16:16).

An added indication that the early church expected a convert to make some statement of faith before receiving baptism is found in Acts 8:37. When the eunuch asks Philip about baptism, Philip replies, "If you believe with all your heart, you may [receive baptism]." The eunuch responds, "I believe that Jesus is the Son of God." This last phrase, the words of the eunuch's confession, are missing in most modern translations and found only in a footnote. That's because the earliest Greek manuscripts don't contain the sentence, and translators believe that later copiers of the Bible added it simply because such a confession had become a common requirement in the church.

Longer Creeds?

If ten words or even three words were an adequate confession for Christians in the early church, why do we have such lengthy creeds, confessions, and formularies today? Isn't "Jesus is Lord" enough of a confession for all Christians?

Yes and no. Yes, in the sense that confessing the risen Lord is all that is necessary for salvation. No, in the sense that as we learn more about God and his church, as we see God's love more clearly, we inevitably look for new words to confess his greatness and to define our faith.

For instance, in the worship service God's people praise his name and confess his greatness through hymns. And most of those hymns are confessions of faith which say publicly who Jesus is and what Christians believe about him. Each author has built on that basic confession, Jesus is Lord, with words that more poetically and completely confess God's greatness. It's not difficult to find the core confession in this hymn from the Bible:

> Great indeed, we confess,
> is the mystery of our religion:
> He was manifested in the flesh,
> vindicated in the Spirit,
> seen by angels,
> preached among the nations,
> believed on in the world,
> taken up in glory.
>
> (1 Tim. 3:16)

Or in John Calvin's hymn:

> I greet Thee, who my sure Redeemer art,
> My only Trust and Savior of my heart.

23

Or in Martin Luther's hymn:

> A might fortress is our God, a bulwark
> never failing;
> our helper he, amid the flood of mortal ills
> prevailing
> . . . Christ Jesus, it is he; Lord Sabbaoth his
> name,
> from age to age the same; and he must win
> the battle.

Or in this contemporary hymn:

> Beautiful Savior! King of creation!
> Son of God and Son of Man!
> Truly I'd love thee, truly I'd serve thee,
> Light of my soul, my joy, my crown.

But worship and praise are not the only reasons for creating and expanding confessions. Sometimes Christians have written confessions to answer denials of certain beliefs. John's first letter describes two such occasions: when people denied the *humanity* of Christ, it became necessary to confess that "Jesus has come in the flesh"; when people denied the *deity* of Jesus, it became necessary to declare that "Jesus is the Son of God" (1 John 4:2, 15).

And that was just the beginning. As the church grew and disagreements flared up, creeds were formulated to settle disputes. The simple statement that Jesus is Lord grew into the Ápostles' Creed, which says that God made us, that Jesus is God and man, that he was born, suffered, died, rose, and rules us, that he is coming again, and that he has given his Spirit to the church.

The Nicene Creed adds more detail, especially on the crucial teaching that Jesus is God. It stresses that he came "for us and for our salvation."

The Athanasian Creed expands the teaching about the Trinity. When this creed was written, this doctrine was so close to the core of the faith that Article 28 says: "He therefore that will be saved must thus think of the Trinity."

Later church confessions, such as the creeds of the Reformation, add more statements on the Bible, the sacraments, salvation by grace, election, and the church.

The setting and purpose of a creed or confession has much to do with its size, detail, and content. For instance, the Heidelberg Catechism was meant to teach—hence its question-and-answer format, its scope from sin to salvation to service, and its warm, comforting tone. The Canons of Dort, with their heavy political overtones, were adopted to settle a theological dispute; thus they are focused sharply on particular questions.

No matter what form or size the church's hymns and creeds of confession take, they all have one thing in common. They are built on a basic statement about Jesus. At the least, the Christian confesses that Jesus is God's Son who became a human being in order to save humankind. But since we know the Father and the Spirit only through the Son, this core statement implies and acknowledges much more. It implies a confession about the Father: he is the Maker of all things; in his love he sent Jesus to redeem his own; he is still with his people through the Spirit. And it acknowledges that we are sinful, that we need Jesus' powerful help, and that we are grateful to Jesus for his help.

But the longer, more complex ways of saying "Jesus is Lord" which have developed over the centuries aren't just examples of modern wordiness. They reflect all that the Spirit by the Word has taught the church during the last nineteen hundred years about this Jesus Christ—who he is and how we should serve him.

The Usefulness of Creeds

In creeds Christians say what they believe. The word *creed* comes from the Latin *credo*, which is the "I believe" with which many creeds start.

Creeds help us recall succinctly the backbone of our faith. We use them to praise God in worship, to teach the faith to young members (note the large slice of the Heidelberg Catechism that is devoted to a study of the Apostles' Creed), and to share the faith with neighbors. When Christians get together to organize a school, a food co-op, or a labor union, they also find it necessary to make a pointed statement of faith to explain why they are undertaking their project.

Creeds are not limited to worship services, church school classes, and the back of hymnbooks. Since they express loyalty to Jesus, the Lord of all of life, and faith in God the Almighty Maker and the ever present Spirit, creeds go with believers throughout life and help them to confess "before men" at many times and places.

As you find opportunity or you are challenged by either questions or denials to state what you believe, you will find the creeds helpful. As you confess again and again, keep Jesus, the Lord, in the center of your confession. Then he and the Father will see to it that ". . . the Holy Spirit, whom the Father will send in [Jesus'] name . . . will teach you all things, and bring to your remembrance all that [Jesus] has said to you" (John 14:26).

STUDY

GUIDE

At Home

1. My questions/comments on chapter three

2. To prepare for the next class session, try writing your own creed. Be sure it contains the minimum statement of belief that anyone wanting to profess his Christian faith should be able to declare. If you have musical or poetical talent, you might try writing a creedal song or poem.

3. As background reading for your creed-writing exercise, study the Form for Public Profession of Faith (Appendix II) and note precisely what the confessor is asked to declare. Also, read Lord's Days 7 through 12 of the Heidelberg Catechism. Lord's Day 7 asks, "What then must a Christian believe?" For a detailed answer to that question, read the Lord's Days which follow.

4. For your devotions this week, read Acts 8:26–39. When Philip explained the words of Isaiah to the Ethiopian eunuch, the eunuch's response was immediate and joyful. He put his confession into words by asking to be baptized. His life rededicated, he went on his way "rejoicing."

   What is your response to Christ's love and how can you live your confession joyfully?

In Class
   1. Is the statement "Jesus is Lord" a sufficient profession of faith? Why or why not?

   2. In small groups, draw up a composite creed. Your instructor will provide the necessary instructions.

   3. How does the following excerpt from *A Place to Stand* (C. Plantinga Jr.) challenge Christians:

      > Ultimately we'll be judged not on the grounds of which confessions we *held*; the Lord will . . . make more of the confessions we *lived*.

      The word-deed nature of a Christian's confession is reflected in Titus 1:16. Can you think of other Scripture passages—or examples from Scripture—which illustrate that creeds are to be spoken and lived?

FOUR

THIS
CHURCH

"You have to keep in mind the era and the town. By Grand Rapids standards, my mother was positively liberal. The Dutch population had two strong church groups, one more strict than the other, and their children weren't allowed to go to the movies, to drive, even to come to the Y to take modern dance lessons."

That's how the Christian Reformed Church of the thirties looked to Mrs. Betty Ford, wife of United States former President Gerald R. Ford. Like Mrs. Ford, moviegoers who have seen *Hardcore* and people who have read Peter DeVries or Frederick Manfred must wonder about this quaint bunch of Dutch Calvinists.

Unfortunately, that's how the Christian Reformed Church is identified—as a group of Dutch Calvinists. Just as people sometimes talk as though all Italians are Roman Catholic, all Germans are Lutheran, all Englishmen are Anglican, and all Scots are Presbyterian, so, people sometimes say, all Dutchmen are Reformed. Such stereotypes, of course, are unfair. They ignore people of these nationalities who belong to other churches or to none at all. And they contradict the character of the church.

The church is not an ethnic group, even though ethnic groups may dominate some churches in certain parts of the world. Nor is the church primarily a social group, even though Ann Landers may correctly say that it's a great place to meet people. The church is a *confessing* community. It's the gathering of people who confess Jesus as their Lord (1 Tim. 3:15, 16).

The word *church* means "of the Lord" or, when it pertains mainly to the adjective *ecclesiastical*, "called out." Therefore class or ethnic origin should never matter in a church. What matters is that Jesus has called the church together and the church must answer his call by obediently holding up his truth.

Church—A Confusing Word

Because people use the word *church* in so many ways, it's often difficult to figure out what they mean:

> "I'm going to church."
> "The church is meeting in the school."
> "I believe the church will last forever."
> "Our church is going to have a new hymnbook soon."

Such statements can be confusing. Is the speaker referring to the building down the street, to a group of people who worship together, to a particular denomination, or to believers of all times and places? The word *church* is often ambiguous.

But perhaps there's good reason for that ambiguity. The small congregation is closely tied to the denomination. And the denomination is an integral part of the universal church. Each *church* (no matter how you understand that word) is a part of the other. Try this exercise. As you think of your local congregation, let your mind wander to other churches in your own city, area, region, county. Then let your mind travel through history: to the church of your grandparents, back to the era of Calvin and Zwingli, to the early New Testament age, and even further back to King David, and to Ruth—to the people who were God's children before the word *church* was ever used. That should give you a pretty good idea of how many groups and people are part of the *church*.

Who We Are

Our particular denomination, just a tiny part of that church universal, is called Christian Reformed. That's a good name because it says a lot about who we are, where we come from, and what we believe. But it's a name most people aren't familiar with. Newspapers often mistakenly refer to us as the Christian "Reform" church, forgetting the "-ed." Others, making the same error, wonder what we're trying to "reform" or if we're somehow tied in with the prison system. When one group of Christian Reformed parents tried to start a school in their town, neighbors quickly protested; they didn't want a "reform" school to lower their property values.

According to the dictionary, *Reformed* means:

> Pertaining to, or designating the body of Protestant churches originating in the Reformation or, in a more restricted sense, of those churches formed in various

European countries by Zwingli, Calvin, and others who separated from Luther on the doctrine of the Lord's Supper. . . .

The adjective *Reformed*, then, describes the origin of the Reformed churches in the Protestant Reformation. More familiar than *Reformed* is the term *Presbyterian*, another adjective which refers to the same group of churches. *Presbyterian* describes the form of church government churches in the Reformed tradition use.

The Christian Reformed Church is just one denomination in the Reformed Presbyterian family of churches. And it has a special character all its own. To understand what's unique about this denomination, we need to consider the church's expression of faith and life and we need to answer some pertinent questions about where we came from, what we believe, and how we operate.

What are our origins? We've been in existence since the mid-1800s. Dutch men and women, fed up with poverty and persecution in the Netherlands, fled to North America. Convinced that they had a unique understanding of the Christian life, these Dutch immigrants—followers of John Calvin—established and maintained their own congregations. From these small congregations grew a denomination—the Christian Reformed Church.

How Do We View the Bible? Some people think the Bible is merely a book humans wrote about God; others respect it as God speaking to humanity or as God-inspired people speaking to humanity. Depending on which of these views you take, the Bible can be an interesting old book, a how-to manual, or the story of human salvation in Jesus Christ.

Reformed Christians share with many others the belief that the Bible is God's Word, spoken to humankind through persons he inspired. Our use of the Bible is perhaps more careful and thorough than most: we view it as the historical record of God's saving deeds by which he calls persons to new life and obedience.

What do we teach about salvation? Some churches teach that people are saved by their own works. Others preach that we are saved only by God's grace. Still others believe that people are saved by a combination of grace and works.

As Reformed Christians we believe we are saved by grace. Therefore, we also believe in election and practice infant baptism, a doctrine and a sacrament which clearly declare that God's grace is first.

How is our church governed? The Roman Catholic Church uses a hierarchical system of church government. The Pope is at the top of the hierarchy. All authority comes from him and is channeled down through cardinals, bishops, and priests.

The Pentecostal church uses a congregational system of church government. Each church runs itself and has few ties with other congregations.

The Christian Reformed Church uses a system which falls somewhere between these two extremes. In the Presbyterian system local congregations and individual members have a voice in church government: they elect deacons, elders, ministers, and evangelists. But each congregation is also part of a regional (classis) and international (synod) network in which and to which it has responsibilities, including the God-given right and authority to discuss, debate, vote, and appeal.

How do we worship? The prescribed form or ritual a church follows for its worship service is called *liturgy*. Churches are sometimes called "high" or "low," depending on what kind of liturgy they use. "High" church services are formal: they incorporate printed liturgies and congregational responses, frequent sacraments, vestments, candles, and other prescribed religious articles. "Low" services are informal: the congregation responds only by singing; there are few sacraments; the pastor usually prefers suit and tie to formal robe; and candles might be used, but only at Christmas.

Each Christian Reformed Church worships a little differently, but most services are a combination of the high and low. Usually the minister reads the Law in the morning service and teaches part of the Heidelberg Catechism in a second service. The sermon is the most prominent part of our worship service.

What is our attitude toward tradition? Do we insist on conserving the old way or do we go quickly and liberally for the new? For the most part, the Christian Reformed Church is on the conservative side. We are slow to adopt new Bible translations or liturgical forms. We do realize, however, that a tradition should not be maintained for tradition's sake alone but must be judged by God's Word (see Heidelberg Catechism, Lord's Day 33).

What is our attitude toward this life? Some people have a this-worldly attitude, hardly talking about or believing in life after death. Others have an other-worldly attitude, waiting for heaven while the world goes to hell. Reformed Christians are neither and both: they serve the Lord in this life, believing it's part of eternal life.

What lifestyle does our church advocate for its members? Reformed Christians are strict in personal lifestyle and radical in Christian living. They view the Christian life not as a Sunday-only matter but as a seven-day-a-week commitment. That commitment demands participation in missions, education, labor, and politics.

Putting It All Together

The above answers give us some idea of what's special about the Christian Reformed Church—how it's different from all the other churches in the yellow pages. Dr. John Kromminga, retired president of Calvin Seminary, describes that distinctiveness this way:

> We are neither liberal nor fundamentalistic. We are a Bible-believing, traditionally and confessionally oriented church. We must function as a Reformed community in today's world. We must know the needs of the world and dare to address them.
>
> There is no easy way to escape that challenge. If we refuse to accept the challenge, even at the cost of making some mistakes, we have ceased to be Reformed.

For Dr. Kromminga, then, to be Reformed means to live what we believe. What the Christian Reformed Church believes is taught in the Bible and confessed in the church's creeds. We share with most Christian churches the three ecumenical creeds: the Apostles', the Nicene, and the Athanasian. But, often in distinction from other churches, the Christian Reformed Church accepts three Reformed confessions: the Heidelberg Catechism, the Belgic Confession, and the Canons of Dort.

The Christian Reformed Church expects its members to know and agree with these statements. That's why, when persons make profession of faith, they are asked:

> Do you believe that the Bible is the Word of God, revealing Christ and his redemption, and that the confessions and proclamations of this church faithfully reflect this revelation?

That's also why most of our churches, in addition to teaching the Heidelberg Catechism in the second service, spend so much time—as much as several years—on it in church school.

Sovereignty

If we were to reach for one word to express what's unique about the Reformed understanding of the Christian faith, that word would be *sovereign*.

We believe that God is sovereign. He is King. He is the power-ful Maker of the world. Because he is the Creator of all that exists, his laws and norms hold for the whole creation. God is *sovereign*; the world belongs to him; it is his kingdom.

Amazingly, this sovereign God created human beings in his likeness. He made them to rule the creation as his stewards and managers. All of us, not only priests and ministers, may and must serve him in all of our living by obeying his laws and directions.

But that's exactly where sin turned us inside out and upside down. Because of sin, human beings do not listen to God; we disobey God arrogantly. We pretend we can manage fine on our own. Even when the mess we have made stares us in the face and doubts stir within, we still minimize our guilt. We begin to wail, "Why doesn't God do something?"

He already has done something! God, in his sovereign grace, chose to save the world. He did this by restoring his kingdom in Jesus and by writing his law on the hearts of believers through his Spirit. By his life, death, and resurrection Jesus became the Savior who paid for our sin; he is the Lord and King of all people. He preached the gospel of the kingdom and taught us to pray for its full coming.

God is as sovereign in salvation as he is in creation. That's good! Sin is so deadening that we wouldn't have a chance if God didn't save us. God's sovereign election of any person who believes in Jesus underscores that grace is grace—it's a free gift!

God is *sovereignly* steady and patient in loving his own. He makes covenants with his people and always keeps his agreements with them.

A Way of Life

Such beliefs radically affect the way believers live. Any person who knows that God is sovereign cannot bow to human rule, either in church or state, that goes against God's will. When we understand and believe that we as individuals are made in this God's likeness, we cannot let a minister do our thinking for us or a priest our worshiping. When we see ourselves as managers for a *sovereign* God, we cannot limit our Christian living to personal piety. Rather, we become concerned about injustice and we seek a renewal of work, education, politics, art, family living, and recreation, through Christ's grace and the Spirit's leading.

Dr. Kromminga has said it's a challenge to be a Reformed Christian. It's exciting to be part of, to share joys and sorrows with, to rest and to work with the group of Christians known as the Christian Reformed Church—not because they are quaint or special, but because the sovereign Creator's grace is at work among them.

STUDY
GUIDE

At Home

1. My questions/comments on chapter four

2. Talk to two confessing members and ask them what it means to be Reformed. Jot down some notes to help you remember what each said and then compare their comments. How do their remarks compare with the ideas in chapter four?

3. For a brief overview of what the Christian Reformed Church is and what it believes, read *Belonging*, a pamphlet by Wilbert M. Van Dyk. If you'd like an in-depth study of the creeds and confessions of the Christian Reformed Church, try Cornelius Plantinga's *A Place to Stand*. For more information on the history of the Christian Reformed Church, read *A Time to Keep* by Herbert Brink and A. James Heynen. Ask your instructor about obtaining these materials.

4. Read the words of the psalmist in Psalm 86:8–13 and of Isaiah in Isaiah 40:18, 28. Both of these passages are tributes to the sovereignty of God. Can you suggest several other passages which speak to you of the absolute rule of our God over all things?

In Class

1. The word *church* is used in many different ways. Read the statements or texts below and describe the sense in which *church* is being used.

    a. "I went to church twice yesterday."

    b. 1 Timothy 3:15, 16

    c. 2 Thessalonians 1:1, 4

    d. The janitor cleans the church on Mondays.

    e. The Second Christian Reformed Church has an effective VBS program.

    f. I don't feel at home in that church.

    g. I believe in a holy catholic church.

Then discuss these questions

a. Are certain uses of the word more legitimate than others? Why?

b. Is it all right to use the word *church* to refer primarily to a building? A congregation? Explain.

2. When a person confesses his faith, he says yes to the following question: "Do you believe that the Bible is the Word of God, revealing Christ and his redemption and that the confessions and proclamations of this church faithfully reflect this revelation?"

a. If someone does not agree with certain articles in one of the confessions, should he answer no to the above question?

b. How much doctrine should a person know before she confesses her faith?

3. Reread Dr. John Kromminga's statement on page 32. The chapter points to *sovereign* as the one word that expresses the uniqueness about the Reformed understanding of Christian faith. How is this word related to what Kromminga says?

What implications do the confession "God is sovereign" and the statement "We must live what we *believe*" have for
　　—what you plan to do on Friday night?
　　—what kind of car you decide to buy?
　　—whether you keep physically fit?
　　—whether you join a union?
　　—whether you join an anti-nuclear demonstration?
　　—how you work out your relationship with your fiancée?
　　—how you use your ability to draw?
　　—whom you vote for in the next campaign for president or prime minister?
　　—how you use language?

4. Role play the following situation:

Two of you are Christian Reformed Church members. You have met two non-Reformed friends at a party and the topic has somehow focused on the Christian Reformed Church and why you attend it. Explain to these two non-Reformed people what it means to be Reformed.

Some tips: Try not to use any jargon which a non-Christian Reformed or non-Reformed person would have difficulty understanding. Think especially of the words *sovereign* and *redeemed*. Can you think of a contemporary metaphor to explain these words?

FIVE

THE PRIVILEGES OF
FULL COMMUNION

In the name of our Lord Jesus Christ I now welcome you to all the privileges of full communion. I welcome you to full participation in the life of the church. I welcome you to its responsibilities, to its privileges, to its joys and its sufferings. May the God of peace . . . .

Form for Public Profession of Faith (Appendix II)

That's the official welcome the church gives to those who profess their faith publicly. It's an acknowledgment that the initial inquiring and learning stage is past (although learning and inquiring must continue throughout life). And it's a welcome to full, mature membership in the church of Jesus Christ.

"Full communion" means more than being allowed to attend the Lord's Supper. When you are welcomed as a member of the church, a number of changes occur. You become *eligible* for official acts and sacraments, and you become responsible for budgets, neighbors, your own actions and those of your church.

Church Order

At first all the new privileges and responsibilities of church membership may seem a little overwhelming. You may wonder how you fit in, what the church expects of you as a new member. You'll find the answers to many of your questions in the Church Order of the Christian Reformed Church. What a rule book is for a sport, the Church Order is for the church. It explains in detail what each of your new privileges and responsibilities entails.

Of course, the Church Order doesn't have the authority of the Bible. It's not an inspired work. It's simply the church's attempt to explain how we think the Lord wants his church to run its

38

day-to-day business. Many of the Church Order's articles aren't even spelled out in the Bible. For example, the Bible doesn't tell us to use the Heidelberg Catechism in the second service or to celebrate Christmas. But the Christian Reformed Church has tried honestly and carefully to make sure each article in the Church Order *agrees* with the Bible. When we discover one that doesn't, we change it.

In the rest of the chapter we'll look at what the Church Order tells us about the *privileges* of full communion. In chapter six we'll examine our new *responsibilities*. You'll discover that the two, privilege and responsibility, often overlap.

Citizenship

One of the privileges of membership in the church is the right to vote. Just as citizens of a nation become eligible to vote when they reach the legal age, so at the time you profess your faith publicly you become eligible to vote at congregational meetings.[1]

Most major decisions about the church's well-being are discussed and voted on at congregational meetings. Members discuss the church's expenses for each fiscal year and vote on a budget. They decide on such things as whether to move to another part of town, whether to build a new building, and whether they should hire someone to shovel snow. They vote for church officers (annually) and a minister (when the need arises). As a member, you are also eligible for election to the offices of elder and deacon.[2]

Sacraments

A very welcome part of full communion is sharing the sacraments with other Christians. The Christian Reformed Church celebrates two sacraments—baptism and the Lord's Supper.

Baptism. We baptize because God promises his salvation to those who answer his grace with their obedience. Baptism (washing one clean with water) symbolizes the forgiveness of sin through Christ's death on the cross.

---

[1]Prior to 1957, full membership for women did not include the privilege of voting. Now, in a majority of Christian Reformed congregations, all full members are eligible to vote at congregational meetings.

[2]Although the church sets no age requirements for holding office (as the state does), it has insisted until quite recently that church officebearers be male. The Synod of 1977 decided that women can serve as deacons.

Unlike many churches, the Christian Reformed Church baptizes infants. We believe and are thankful that in his mercy God includes children in his covenant (Gen. 17:7, *descendants*; Acts 2:39, *your children*). If you were baptized as an infant, and if you are now thinking about professing your faith publicly, you no doubt see in your own life how God sticks to his word. Your parents and the church taught you about the Lord. Now it's up to you to respond to God's covenant offer to be your God.

If you were not baptized as an infant, you will be baptized when you publicly profess your faith. And God makes that same covenant offer to you. That's the marvel of God's grace—it's not just for insiders. Peter said at Pentecost, ". . . For the promise is to you and to your children and to all that are far off, everyone whom the Lord our God calls to him" (Acts 2:39). The *far off* are the non-Jews, the Gentiles—and that's us. That's how most of us are included in God's salvation. God reaches out with his gospel beyond borders and ethnic accents. And he welcomes all those who come to him in faith.

Lord's Supper. Full membership also includes participation in the Lord's Supper, so called because Christ himself initiated this sacrament. We hear communion forms, annual sermons (when the topic comes up in the Heidelberg Catechism), and preparatory and applicatory sermons before and after each celebration of the Lord's Supper. But new members are often still confused by it all. They come to their first communion with high expectations, and sometimes, regrettably, they do not get what they expect. Some wonder, "Am I doing this right?"

Here are three things to keep in mind. First, Jesus said: "Do this in remembrance of me." Therefore the most obvious thing to do as you hold the bread or wait for the wine to be passed is to *remember*. Think about Jesus, especially about his death, as symbolized by the broken bread and the poured wine. Remember: his death. . .your life! Contrast: your sin. . .his love! That remembering alone, with the elements of the sacrament in your hand, will bring you closer to him.

Second, think of the surprising words Paul said about the supper. You may have heard the words often, but don't let that dull their meaning for you personally.

> For as often as you eat this bread and drink the cup,
> you proclaim the Lord's death until he comes (1 Cor. 11:26).

You proclaim! The word as used in the Greek means "preach." At the Lord's table you and the whole church are preaching. Think about it. What are you preaching? ". . .the

Lord's death until he comes." Each time you participate in the sacrament you are saying publicly: the Lord died, he died for me, he rose victoriously, and he is coming back! Therefore, even if you were to get nothing else from the sacrament, you have reprofessed your faith.

The third thought is less celebrative, more sobering. Every professing Christian knows, but sometimes forgets, the danger of judgment when one "eats and drinks without discerning the body" (1 Cor. 11:29). That means that we should *see* "the body" in the sacrament, the body of Christ dying on the cross for us, his church with its needs and failures.

Not everyone should come to the Lord's Supper. A person must know enough about Jesus to know what's happening in the sacrament. One should also be committed enough to Jesus to let the fellowship at the table function in all of life:

> You cannot drink the cup of the Lord and the cup of demons. You cannot partake of the table of the Lord and the table of demons. Shall we provoke the Lord to jealousy? (1 Cor. 10:21, 22)

Church Papers

If you move one day to another church or another city, you may have your membership ("papers") transferred to another Christian Reformed Church as a communicant member; you needn't publicly profess your faith again.

Also, if you are visiting friends in another congregation on a day in which they have communion, you will be welcome to join with them in their celebration. Churches have different methods of asking you to identify yourself and of welcoming you. In some churches you will be welcomed by an elder or two and your name may be read publicly; in others you may be asked to fill in a card and you will be introduced to the congregation. A warm welcome intensifies the oneness you will experience with the host congregation at the Lord's Supper. It helps you remember you are part of the *church*, the church which is so much larger than one congregation!

STUDY

GUIDE

At Home
   1. My questions/comments on chapter five

2. Turn to the Church Order (Appendix I) and indicate what privileges confessing members claim in each of the following Articles:
   —Article 3

   —Article 4c

   —Article 37

   —Article 57

   —Article 59

   —Article 66

3. For your additional reading and reflection this week study the Form for the Lord's Supper most often used by your congregation.

   If you're interested in examining the scriptural base for the Church Order, try Cornelius Plantinga Jr.'s *A Place to Stand*, chapter 23. Chapter 24 of this book, especially pages 116–118, provides deeper insights into the Christian Reformed Church's approach to the sacraments.

4. The classic passage on the Lord's Supper, which is quoted in all the forms, is 1 Corinthians 11:23–29. Take time this week to reflect on this Scripture.

In Class
1. Consider these situations involving the Church Order:

   Carol wonders whether she should profess her faith even though she does not agree with Article 3 of the Christian Reformed Church Order. She believes that the church, in failing to encourage women to use their talents in office, is not completely faithful to Scripture.

   Kurt questions why the Church Order designates certain privileges for confessing members only. He wonders where the Bible spells out these restrictions.

a. What are the two basic principles on which the Church Order depends? (See Appendix III, C.)

b. How would you answer Carol and Kurt?

2. Using this chapter's section on the Lord's Supper, discuss the words *remember, proclaim,* and *commune.* With others in your group, try to reach a consensus of what each term means to the person participating in the Lord's Supper.

3. What are some of the expectations, difficulties, and questions you have about participating in the Lord's Supper? Do you look forward to participation? Do you feel comfortable with the way the supper is celebrated in your church? Does anything bother you or frighten you about participating?

SIX

THE RESPONSIBILITIES
OF FULL COMMUNION

When we looked at the meaning of "full communion" in the previous chapter, we concentrated on the privileges and rights of membership in the Christian Reformed Church. This chapter focuses on responsibilities.

Gifts of Money

Long ago when all of North America belonged to the British Empire, the colonists in Boston staged a tea party to protest taxes imposed on colonies who had very little say in their governing. The colonists' slogan was "No taxation without representation." And they had a good point. Membership in any organization or institution carries with it the responsibility of financial support. But it usually also guarantees the privilege of speaking out or voting.

Some churches are as guilty as the British Empire was of ignoring the voice of the people—but Reformed and Presbyterian congregations are not among them. As a member of the Christian Reformed Church you may vote for officebearers, approve or reject the proposed budget, express your opinion on important issues, and take a proposal or question to classis or synod if you think the local church is in error.

Along with this right to vote, of course, comes the responsibility to "put your money where your mouth is." Most churches need a sizable regular contribution from each member for salaries and operating expenses, building costs, and worldwide ministries.

The Christian Reformed Church supports worldwide ministries through a *quota* system. Each congregation is asked to pay $400 to $500 per family for world missions, broadcasting, home missions, church education, and mutual church help. The Christian Reformed Church World Relief Committee also encourages its members to give another one percent of their income for the fight against world hunger. And many classes ask for regional support for such programs as a campus ministry in Ann Arbor, Michigan, or a ministry to native people in Regina, Saskatchewan.

If, before public profession, you have been nickel-and-diming the Sunday offering, the expected weekly budget will look like quite a sum. But, compared to the price of a tank of gas, it's not so bad. After all, you'll get great mileage in terms of caring for and helping people. And because the Christian Reformed Church Synod carefully scrutinizes each quota cause, you can be sure your gifts are *rightly* used for significant work in a needy world.

Gifts of Praise

The most important gift you can give God is the gift of praise. That's why the church asks its members to worship together regularly:

> The congregation shall assemble for worship at least twice on the Lord's Day to hear God's Word, to receive the sacraments, to engage in praise and prayer, and to present gifts of gratitude.
> Church Order, Article 51a (Appendix I)

One thing which sets us off from many other denominations is our second service. The pattern of two services goes back to a decision made at the Synod of Dort in the 1600s. We have traditionally held one service for proclaiming the Word and another for "preaching the Word as summarized in the Heidelberg Catechism" (Church Order, Article 54).

Not all Christian Reformed churches follow this pattern exactly, but all do believe that gathering together twice on Sunday is important. The council or consistory arranges our worship services; as members, it is our responsibility to attend:

> . . . and let us consider how to stir up one another to love and good works, not neglecting to meet together, as is the habit of some, but encouraging one another, and all the more as you see the Day drawing near.
> Hebrews 10:24, 25

Witnessing

It's often tempting to avoid our responsibility to witness. Witnessing makes us uneasy and sometimes unpopular. Besides, we support our church's mission and evangelism programs—

isn't that enough? Let trained preachers and teachers do the witnessing.

No, says the apostle Peter, that's not enough. *All* Christians must "declare the wonderful deeds of him who called you out of darkness into his marvelous light" (1 Pet. 2:9). All Christians must be ready to give a good explanation "to any one who calls you to account for the hope that is in you" (1 Pet. 3:15). We are "to be witnesses for Christ in word and deed" (Church Order, Article 73).

And why not? A man who drives a diesel Rabbit is eager to praise the fuel economy. A woman who is into windsurfing can't quit talking about the wind and the waves. May not Jesus —our Maker, Savior, and Lord—expect that his children be so taken by what he does and has done for them that they will talk about it easily and walk his way gladly? That's exactly what witnessing is—declaring his deeds and talking about the hope he has placed in our hearts.

So why do Christians sometimes seem so scared to witness? Probably because they think they have to use the Jehovah's Witness approach: door to door, two by two, rude and inconvenient, managing a tight smile when another door is slammed.

Actually, there are many ways to witness. Each of us may speak, in word or deed, about Jesus in our own way. Some may witness by befriending a person who's lonely, others by hospital visiting or door-to-door calling. Some may have natural gifts for telling the good news while others will want to take a course or enroll in an evangelism training program. The important thing is that we recognize that all approaches to witnessing are not and need not be alike and that we trust the Holy Spirit to help each of us confess Jesus as Lord.

Encouragement

Team sports create a lot of chatter from the bench and on the field. Players encourage each other to do well and to not be discouraged by a couple of errors or fumbles. A team that stops encouraging and begins knocking fellow players is usually a losing team.

The church is also an encouraging fellowship. The call to encourage comes in the New Testament (Heb. 10:24; Phil. 2:1–4). In actual practice we answer this call through fellowship meetings, visits, phone calls, and, surprisingly, even through discipline:

> The exercise of admonition and discipline by the consistory does not preclude the responsibility of the

believers to watch over and to admonish one another in love.

Church Order, Article 78b (Appendix I)

It takes tact and love to admonish other Christians, but it's worth the effort. Without that concern, without that love, the church would be like a family that's not on speaking terms.

Participation

When Ellen White joined the church, she didn't think she had much to offer. And she didn't really understand what it meant to take part in the full life and work of the church. She was content to be a "pew-sitter" and to let "them" take care of everything.

Almost a year after her welcome, Ellen attended her first congregational meeting. The council distributed mimeographed sheets listing all the many classes and ministries in which members could become involved and asked each person present to commit himself to one or two activities. Ellen was surprised at the number of choices she had—and many of them looked interesting! There were several adult classes and discussion groups, a task force who raised money for world hunger, and another group who went to the jail twice a month to lead services. Although she didn't feel qualified to teach, Ellen was happy to note that the church also needed classroom helpers, nursery attendants, and someone to gather materials for crafts. Suddenly Ellen had discovered many ways in which she could contribute; she had no trouble at all making her commitment.

Like Ellen, each of us has to overcome our reluctance to serve and our willingness to let someone else run things. We must be willing to learn, to befriend others, to make proposals, and to use our time and skills. It's our responsibility to participate.

Discipline

Discipline is a scary and unpleasant term for something we've been doing since childhood. Think of the kid on third base or on the end of the skipping rope who didn't get with it and show some effort. How long before the others began to rumble that they'd be better off without him?

That's the kind of discipline most of us are familiar with. But that's not the kind of discipline we use in Christ's name in the church. True, we exclude a member because he no longer shares the church's goals, work, lifestyle, or beliefs. But long before we exclude him, we work—through a network of caring, supporting relationships—to keep him in. And even after we exclude him, we try hard to bring him back.

It's for that very reason that we seldom hear public announcements of discipline. Often disciplined members either leave the church before the public announcement can be made or—and we praise God that this happens regularly—they repent.

Many times discipline is the last resort. Like a fire, trouble can begin with a trivial, minor, or, in some cases, a serious incident. Because of lack of communication between member and minister or consistory, or because of distorted communication and gossip, the trouble and the pain are magnified.

As you consider taking that important step, profession of faith, you should make a promise to *yourself* and the church. Promise yourself now that if you should ever be in trouble, or if you should disagree with something in the church, you will talk about it with your elder or your pastor.

Too often a member gradually disappears from the scene. When someone finally catches up with her, it's almost too late; bridges have been burned, a new pattern has been set.

Members of the church, and especially your elder and pastor, cannot always know that you are hurting if you don't tell them. So please do! It hurts us when a member fades away.

STUDY GUIDE

At Home
1. My questions/comments on chapter six

2. List as many of your church's programs and activities as you can under the appropriate headings below. For example, Calvinette and Cadet clubs might be part of your educational program, and family visitation might be part of the pastoral program.

Programs
of
_____
(name of your church)

Pastoral

Evangelistic

Educational

Diaconal

How much do you know about each of these programs? Are you or have you been involved in any? Would you like to be? Are there new activities you'd like to see made available?

3. Read Appendix III, section B to learn about the CRWRC's World Hunger Fund. The Christian Reformed Church's goal is that each family give one percent of its income to this cause. Is this goal being reached in your church?

4. 1 Peter 4:7–11 is an eloquent little summary of the need for church members to love one another. As you reflect on this passage this week, think about ways you can be hospitable and encouraging, using your gifts to serve others.

In Class

1. After watching or listening to the presentation about our denominational ministries, do you have any questions or comments?

2. With others in your class, make a composite list of your congregation's activities, using the same grid you completed at home. Which activities interest you? What gifts can you put to use in kingdom activities? Any questions about your church's activities are sincerely invited.

3. Peter, a plumber, makes $28,000 a year. He is paying off his $12,000 Camaro and is saving money to build a house. Julie, his fiancée, works parttime and earns $8,000 a year, but she must return to school fulltime to finish her degree in social work.

   Peter and Julie plan to marry within a year. They would like to save as much money as possible, but they have also been discussing what percentage of their incomes they should give to the church. Julie and Peter have asked you, their friend, for advice.

   What advice would you give them? How should they decide what to give to the church? What factors should they consider?

4. How can discipline be looked at positively?

SEVEN

READY TO BE
WELCOMED

We've come to the final chapter of this book and the last session of the course. You and other class members have read and thought and talked about confessing your faith in Jesus Christ. But where do you go from here? Are you ready to confess your faith publicly?

Reluctant?

We hope you are ready, that you are eager to make plans for public confession. But if you're still a little uncertain, don't be discouraged. Some reluctance and remaining questions are very understandable. Public profession of faith is a significant step—that's why you've been discussing it for seven weeks. You should not take the step lightly. Nor should you profess your faith just because you've put some time into these sessions and think people expect you to "graduate."

The significance of saying, "Yes, I believe," before the church can be compared to the vows people made in Old Testament times. In an emergency or as a special act of thanksgiving the Israelites often made solemn promises to God. But they were warned not to make promises they couldn't keep:

> When you vow a vow to God, do not delay in paying
> it; for he has no pleasure in fools. Pay what you vow.
> It is better that you should not vow than that you
> should vow and not pay.
>
> (Eccles. 5:4, 5)

What Am I Waiting For?

Since the words people say when they confess their faith in front of the church do count very much, you might wonder whether you're really ready to take this step. Should you go ahead or wait a little longer? That's a question you'll have to answer yourself.

Of course, if you don't believe that Jesus is the Son of God, or if you're not ready to commit your life to Jesus' rule, then it would be dishonest and foolish to try to please your parents or your friends by pretending. Even if you do believe with all your heart, you might have some doubts. You might be thinking you should know and feel and do more before you confess your faith publicly.

If you're struggling with these kinds of questions, listen to the confession of a father who wanted Jesus to heal his son. "Do you believe?" Jesus asked him. "I believe; help my unbelief!" he answered (Mark 9:24). You or I might have been tempted to tell the man to go home and make up his mind—quit the doubletalk. But not Jesus: he healed the man's son. When people know enough to go to Jesus for help even with their unbelief, they are on the right track.

Remember that when you confess Jesus as your Lord, Jesus himself echoes your confession before God (Matt. 10:32). You will not be alone in front of the church. Nor will you be alone later when hard testing comes your way. Jesus will always be with you, and he sends his Spirit to help you.

What Will "They" Ask Me?

Confessing one's faith takes a lifetime. One stage of that confession, the one that concerns you now, is that interview with the consistory.

What will they ask? Will it be a comprehensive exam of everything you've ever learned in church? Must you, will you, meet the *whole* consistory? Will you be on your own or will you be with a group? Does anyone ever fail?

The questions in the Church Order (Appendix I, Article 59) and the Form for Public Profession (Appendix II) give you a good idea of what the consistory will want to discuss. They'll ask why you want to become a full member of the church, what you believe, how you have been serving, and how you intend to serve our Lord.

If you still have worries, ask your pastor what to expect. You'll discover that most consistory members find these interviews very happy occasions. They look forward to meeting members who want to confess their faith. They are eager to hear the witness and testimony of maturing and new members. Consistory members do not give anyone a hard time.

What Am I To Say?

A note included with the Christian Reformed Church 1972 Form for Public Profession of Faith (Appendix II) says this:

> The questions may be changed into statements and said by the confessors. Opportunity may also be given here for additional self-expression on the part of the confessors. When the number of confessors is large the response may be asked of each after the last question only.

What that means is that there's no prescribed format for the ceremony of public profession. There's no rule that says all you may say is "yes" or "I do." Perhaps you'll want to tell the congregation about a striking event in your life, sing a song, or say the questions aloud as statements. Some groups (and/or individuals) plan the service with their pastor, selecting hymns and Scripture passages and helping with the readings and prayers.

Do give some thought to what you are willing to do in this special church service. When you become a full member, you are expected to put your skills to work in the church—and this is a good time to start!

And What If I'm Not Ready?

This course was planned to help you explore what it means to confess your faith publicly. If at this point you are not ready to confess your faith, don't feel that you've failed. Your hesitancy may well show honesty and growth in self-knowledge and for that you are to be respected.

However, it might be valuable to analyze your position. In the light of the discussions in this book, can you define what's holding you back? Do you feel you don't know enough about this church? Do you disagree with some of its teachings or dislike some of its practices? Do you find the way of salvation unclear? Do you want to study the Bible more? Do you have trouble seeing yourself serving Jesus in all you do? Does the grass look greener somewhere else?

Think carefully about your reasons for waiting longer. Once you've defined them somewhat, invite your pastor for a chat or go to his study. Maybe you can work together on the questions or uneasy feelings you have. There are also books you can read, courses you might take, work you could do, and other Christians you can talk to about your doubts.

Don't despair, though, convinced that you'll never find the seemingly easy trust in God that others have, for God has said:

> You will seek me and find me; when you seek me with all your heart. (Jer. 29:13)

> Draw near to God and he will draw near to you. (James 4:8)

Keep searching; you will find!

After the Vows

Why have we spent seven weeks talking about a ceremony that usually only takes about ten minutes? Because public profession works in the life of the Christian something like marriage vows work in the lives of a husband and wife. When you confess your faith before the church, you vow—in much the same way as a man and woman vow at their wedding—to live a life of commitment and obedience to Jesus. Although that life may be filled with challenges and struggles and your faith may often be tested, you can count on lasting joy and peace. The life you live, with God and his Son Jesus, is eternal life now (John 17:2–3).

STUDY GUIDE

At Home

1. My questions/comments on chapter seven and/or this course

Preparing for Discussion

2. If you feel ready to profess your faith, share your decision with someone. Keep praying about it, too, asking God to strengthen you.

   If you do not feel ready to profess your faith, share that decision with someone too. Reflect on or discuss what has to happen or change so that you can be ready. You might list these changes on paper. Continue to pray that God will give you wisdom as you decide.

3. If you'd like to learn more about the church, your instructor can help you obtain the following books:

   A Place to Stand—an extensive study of our creeds and confessions

   Beyond Doubt—daily devotions and helps to Christian living

   Reasons—a study of various cults, objections to the Christian faith, and the distinctiveness of the Reformed faith

   Belonging—a description of the Christian Reformed Church and its beliefs

4. As we struggle to find faith and to put it into practice, it's good to know that God is at work in us (Phil. 2:13). Read the first thirteen verses of Philippians 2 for your devotions this week.

In Class

1. What reasons might people have for wanting to confess their faith? What reasons might they have for deciding to wait? What reasons do you have for wanting or waiting to profess?

2. You have often discussed the relationship of faith to your daily living. Whether you plan to confess your faith publicly at the end of this course or not, Mark 9:35 makes a provocative statement to believers: "You want to be first? Then you better figure on being last. And you better be everybody's servant" (paraphrase).

   Do you find that statement contradictory? How does such a statement work out in the church?

3. The rest of the class time may be spent in helping those class members who wish to make public profession. The contributions of all class members—whether planning to profess or not—are sincerely requested.

   a. Do you have questions about or for the consistorial interview?

   b. Study the questions in the Form for Public Profession of Faith (Appendix II). Discuss with the class how you would like to answer them. Do you want to respond with a simple *yes* or *no*? Would you rather say the questions as statements or write up your own confession?

   c. Are there any Scripture passages, hymns, or other special requests you would like to have included in the service? Do you have suggestions for any part of the service, such as a specific text for the minister's sermon, specific hymns, or a responsive reading?

   d. Would you personally (or as a class) like to respond to your confession with a song, statement, or prayer?

   e. When do you prefer to have the profession of faith service take place?

APPENDIX I

Selected Articles from the Christian Reformed Church Order

Introduction

Article 1

a. The Christian Reformed Church, confessing its complete subjection to the Word of God and the Reformed creeds as a true interpretation of this Word, acknowledging Christ as the only head of his church, and desiring to honor the apostolic injunction that in the churches all things are to be done decently and in order (1 Cor. 14:40), regulates its ecclesiastical organization and activities in the following articles.

b. The main subjects treated in this Church Order are: The Offices of the Church, The Assemblies of the Church, The Task and Activities of the Church, and The Admonition and Discipline of the Church.

Article 3

a. Confessing male members of the church who meet the biblical requirements are eligible for the offices of minister, elder, and evangelist.

b. All confessing members of the church who meet the biblical requirements are eligible for the office of deacon.

c. Only those who have been officially called and ordained or installed shall hold and exercise office in the church.

—Cf. Supplement, Article 3

Article 4

a. In calling and electing to an office, the council shall

ordinarily present to the congregation a nomination of at least twice the number to be elected. When the council submits a nomination which totals less than twice the number to be elected, it shall give reasons for doing so.

b. Prior to making nominations the consistory may give the congregation an opportunity to direct attention to suitable persons.

c. The election by the congregation shall take place under the supervision of the consistory after prayer and in accordance with the regulations established by the consistory. The right to vote shall be limited to confessing members in good standing.

d. After having called the elected persons to their respective offices and having announced their names, the consistory shall proceed to ordain or install them if no valid impediment has arisen. The ordination or installation shall take place in the public worship services with the use of the prescribed ecclesiastical forms.

Article 37

The council, besides seeking the cooperation of the congregation in the election of officebearers, shall also invite its judgment about other major matters, except those which pertain to the supervision and discipline of the congregation. For this purpose the council shall call a meeting at least annually of all members entitled to vote. Such a meeting shall be conducted by the council, and only those matters which it presents shall be considered. Although full consideration shall be given to the judgment expressed by the congregation, the authority for making and carrying out final decisions remains with the consistory as the governing body of the church.

Article 51

a. The congregation shall assemble for worship at least twice on the Lord's day to hear God's Word, to receive the sacraments, to engage in praise and prayer, and to present gifts of gratitude.

b. Worship services shall be held in observance of Christmas, Good Friday, Easter, Ascension Day, and Pentecost, and ordinarily on Old and New Year's Day, and annual days of prayer and thanksgiving.

c. Special worship services may be proclaimed in times of great stress or blessing for church, nation, or world.

Article 56

The covenant of God shall be sealed to children of believers by holy baptism. The consistory shall see to it that baptism is requested and administered as soon as feasible.

Article 57

Adults who have not been baptized shall receive holy baptism upon public profession of faith. The form for the Baptism of Adults shall be used for such public professions.

Article 59

a. Members by baptism shall be admitted to the Lord's Supper upon a public profession of Christ according to the Reformed creeds, with the use of the prescribed form. Before the profession of faith the consistory shall examine them concerning their motives, doctrine, and conduct. The names of those who are to be admitted to the Lord's Supper shall be announced to the congregation for approval at least one Sunday before the public profession of faith.

b. Confessing members coming from other Christian Reformed congregations shall be admitted to communicant membership upon the presentation of certificates of membership attesting their soundness in doctrine and life.

c. Confessing members coming from churches in ecclesiastical fellowship shall be admitted to communicant membership upon presentation of certificates or statements of membership after the consistory has satisfied itself concerning the doctrine and conduct of the members. Persons coming from other denominations shall be admitted to communicant membership only after the consistory has examined them concerning doctrine and conduct. The consistory shall determine in each case whether to admit them directly or by public reaffirmation or profession of faith. Their names shall be announced to the congregation for approval.

Article 66

a. Confessing members who remove to another Christian Reformed church are entitled to a certificate, issued by the consistory, concerning their doctrine and life. When such certificates of membership are requested, they shall ordinarily be mailed to the church of their new residence.

b. Members by baptism who remove to another Christian Reformed church shall upon proper request be granted a certificate of baptism, to which such notations as are necessary shall be attached. Such certificates shall as a rule be mailed to the church of their new residence.

c. Ecclesiastical certificates shall be signed by the president and clerk of the consistory.

Article 73

a. In obedience to Christ's Great Commission, the churches must bring the gospel to all men at home and abroad, in order to lead them into fellowship with Christ and his church.

b. In fulfilling this mandate, each council shall stimulate the members of the congregation to be witnesses for Christ in word and deed, and to support the work of home and foreign missions by their interest, prayers, and gifts.

Article 78

a. The admonition and discipline of the church are spiritual in character and therefore require the use of spiritual means.

b. The exercise of admonition and discipline by the consistory does not preclude the responsibility of the believers to watch over and to admonish one another in love.

Article 80

All members of the congregation are subject in both doctrine and life to the admonition and discipline of the church.

Article 83

a. Members by baptism who willfully neglect to make public profession of faith, or are delinquent in doctrine or life, and do not heed the admonitions of the consistory shall be dealt with in accordance with the regulations of synod and, if they persist in their sin, shall be excluded from the church of Christ.

b. Members by baptism who have been excluded from the church and who later repent of their sin shall be received again into the church only upon public profession of faith.

Article 86

a. Confessing members who have been barred from the Lord's Supper and who after repeated admonitions show no signs of repentance shall be excommunicated from the church of Christ. The Form for Excommunication shall be used for this purpose.

b. The consistory, before excommunicating anyone, shall make three announcements in which the nature of the offense and the obstinacy of the sinner are explained and the congregation is urged to pray for him and to admonish him. In the first announcement the name of the sinner shall ordinarily be withheld but may be mentioned at the discretion of the consistory. In the second, after the classis has given its approval to proceed with further discipline, his name shall be mentioned. In the third, the congregation shall be informed that unless the sinner repents he will be excommunicated on a specified date.

APPENDIX II

Public Profession of Faith

Congregation of our Lord Jesus Christ:

Today we are privileged to welcome into the full life of the church's fellowship those who wish to confess their faith in Christ as Lord and Savior. When they were baptized God made clear his claim on them as his own, and they were received into the church. Now they wish to share fully in the life of this congregation and of the whole church of God. And so today they will publicly accept and confirm what was sealed in their baptism, confess their faith in the Lord Jesus, and offer themselves to God as his willing servants. We thank God for having given them this desire and pray that as we now hear their confession, he will favor us with the presence and guidance of his Holy Spirit.

*The Vows**

_____(name)_____, will you stand now, and in the presence of God and his people respond to the following questions:

1. Do you believe that Jesus Christ is the Son of God sent to redeem the world, do you love and trust him as the one who saves you from your sin, and do you with repentance and joy embrace him as Lord of your life?

Answer: I do.

---

*The questions may be changed into statements and said by the confessors. Opportunity may also be given here for additional self-expression on the part of the confessors. The response may be asked after the last question only.

2. Do you believe that the Bible is the Word of God revealing Christ and his redemption, and that the confessions of this church faithfully reflect this revelation?

Answer: I do.

3. Do you accept the gracious promises of God sealed to you in your baptism and do you affirm your union with Christ and his church which your baptism signifies?

Answer: I do.

4. Do you promise to do all you can with the help of the Holy Spirit, to strengthen your love and commitment to Christ by sharing faithfully in the life of the church, honoring and submitting to its authority; and do you join with the people of God in doing the work of the Lord everywhere?

Answer: I do.

The Reception

[The minister asks the congregation to rise.]

Minister: In the name of our Lord Jesus Christ I now welcome you to all the privileges of full communion. I welcome you to full participation in the life of the church. I welcome you to its responsibilities, its joys, and its sufferings. "May the God of peace, who through the blood of the eternal covenant brought back from the dead our Lord Jesus, that great Shepherd of the sheep, equip you with everything good for doing his will, and may he work in us what is pleasing to him, through Jesus Christ, to whom be glory for ever and ever. Amen." (*Heb. 13:20–21*).

Congregation: Thanks be to God! We promise you our love, encouragement, and prayers.

Minister: Let us together say what we believe: *[Here follows the Apostles' Creed in unison.]*

The Prayer

Lord, our God, we thank you for your Word and Spirit through which we know Jesus Christ as Lord and Savior. May those who confessed your name today never cease to wonder at what you have done for them. Help them to continue firmly in the faith, to bear witness to your love, and to let the Holy Spirit shape their lives. Take them, good Shepherd, into your care that they may loyally endure opposition in serving you.

May we, with all your children, live together in the joy and power of your Holy Spirit. We ask this, Lord Jesus, in the hope of your coming. Amen.

APPENDIX III

SECTION A

John Calvin's Comments on Profession of Faith

True Confirmation

How I wish that we might have kept the custom which, as I have said, existed among the ancient Christians before this misborn wraith of a sacrament came to birth! Not that it would be a confirmation such as they fancy, which cannot be named without doing injustice to baptism; but a catechizing, in which children or those near adolescence would give an account of their faith before the church. But the best method of catechizing would be to have a manual drafted for this exercise, containing and summarizing in simple manner most of the articles of our religion, on which the whole believers' church ought to agree without controversy. A child of ten would present himself to the church to declare his confession of faith, would be examined in each article, and answer to each; if he were ignorant of anything or insufficiently understood it, he would be taught. Thus, while the church looks on as a witness, he would profess the one true and sincere faith, in which the believing folk with one mind worship the one God.

If this discipline were in effect today, it would certainly arouse some slothful parents, who carelessly neglect the instruction of their children as a matter of no concern to them; for then they could not overlook it without public disgrace. There would be greater agreement in faith among Christian people, and not so many would go untaught and ignorant; some would not be so rashly carried away with new and strange doctrines; in short, all would have some methodical instruction, so to speak, in Christian doctrine.

66

From John Calvin, *Institutes of the Christian Religion*, Book 4, Chapter 19, Paragraph 13. The Westminster Press, Philadelphia, copyright 1960.

APPENDIX III

SECTION B

1% For World Hunger

What can you buy with $15? An inexpensive magazine subscription? A modest restaurant meal for a family? In some places in the world, $15 is enough to buy food for a family for a month!

Fifteen dollars is also about 1% of the monthly income of many people in North America. (For some, of course, $15 is more than 1%, and for others it's less.)

Can you spare 1% of your income for hunger relief? That's what our Synod has recommended as a target. And the 1% should, said Synod, be given "without a decrease in contributions to other work of the Kingdom." Will you consider it?

There certainly is need. At least 500 million of the world's people suffer hunger, according to the United Nations. Some are starving and near death; most are malnourished. A billion more have barely enough money for food. What's left over may go for clothing and medicine: maybe an occasional "luxury" like a radio. Even in the US and Canada hunger exists: emergency food kitchens have plenty of patrons.

We're blessed by God with the means—and the opportunity—to help. Sometimes we don't feel like there's anything to spare. But it could be because our standard for what's "enough" is so high. And we have the habit of comparing our lifestyles with those richer than we, not poorer.

If 1% giving is important and within our means, what's the best way to do it? We might consider treating it like the tithe, putting the money aside first, then making whatever adjustments may be necessary. Or we might try making a schedule for gradually working up to the 1% level.

However it's done, some sacrifice may be necessary, perhaps of a smoking habit, one fast-food meal a month, or even something more consequential. The important questions are: "Is giving 1% important and is it needed?" and "Does God want this from me?" If the answers are "yes," the belt-tightening may be uncomfortable, but there are also these trustworthy words: "Give to the poor and you will never be in need." (Prov. 28:27, TEV)

One-percent gifts may be placed in specially designated envelopes and sent directly to CRWRC or put in the church offering plate. The money goes to help malnourished people in Sierra Leone—site of our church's Special Hunger Project—and other countries where hunger is a long-term problem. (The donor specifies where.) The funds support programs in which the Christian Reformed Church is proclaiming and demonstrating God's love—with long-term solutions.

APPENDIX III

SECTION C

Polity of the Christian Reformed Church

Introduction—Reformed Church Polity

The Christian Reformed Church in North America, in harmony with the Word of God and the Reformed creeds as an interpretation of that Word, acknowledges Jesus Christ as the only head and ruler of the church. To carry out his rule the church has adopted a Church Order so that all things in the church may be done decently and in order (1 Cor. 14:40). The general pattern of the organization provided by the Church Order is presbyterian: that is, a system of leadership by elders (presbyters) who represent Christ in his church. Reformed church polity is not strictly presbyterian in all respects, however, and differs in approach from traditional presbyterian polity in that the polity of Reformed churches, while regulative, is not confessional in nature; that is, the Reformed Church Order does not have the status of a creed.

Reformed churches have never claimed that every detail of their system is determined by the Scriptures. Only certain basic principles are found there, providing general directions to the church. Details may and do vary from one Reformed family of churches to another because expediency and specific circumstances often require varying approaches.

Church polity is not—and should not be made into—a fixed, rigid system of rules. Whenever the profit of the churches requires, the specific application of the general principles derived from Scripture must be changed. In a previous version of its Church Order the Christian Reformed Church expressed this in the following way: "The Articles...have been so drafted and adopted by common consent, that they (if the profit of the Church demand otherwise) *may and ought to be*

70

altered, augmented, or diminished." There is, as a result, an amazing amount of flexibility in procedures and practices possible within the polity of the Christian Reformed Church.

From *Manual of Christian Reformed Church Government* by William P. Brink and Richard R. De Ridder, Board of Publications of the Christian Reformed Church, 1979.